BOUQUET FOR GRANDMOTHER

An Arrangement of Stories, Meditations, and Biblical Inspirations

SUSAN B. TOWNSEND

Avon, Massachusetts

Published by Adams Media, an F+W Publications Company
57 Littlefield Street
Avon, MA 02322
www.adamsmedia.com

ISBN-10: 1-59869-150-3
ISBN-13: 978-1-59869-150-4

Printed in the United States of America.
J I H G F E D C B A

Library of Congress Cataloging-in-Publication Data
A bouquet for grandmother / [compiled by] Susan B. Townsend.
p. cm.
ISBN-13: 978-1-59869-150-4 (pbk.)
ISBN-10: 1-59869-150-3 (pbk.)
1. Grandmothers—Anecdotes. 2. Grandmothers—Quotations.
I. Townsend, Susan
HQ759.9.B685 2007
306.874'5—dc22   2007015784

Dedication

In loving memory of my grandmother
Maidie Christina Armstrong.
1898–1986

Acknowledgments

My heartfelt thanks go to:

The people at Adams Media for giving me this wonderful opportunity.

My editor, Paula Munier, for being smart, funny, and beautiful.

My Aunt Helen for indulging my passion for stories.

My brothers and sisters at Sussex Baptist Church for their love, friendship, and unwavering loyalty.

Zella, Jeanie, Gabriel, Rosalie, Steve, Krys, Brandy, Jenny, Wayne, Peggy, and LaRose for allowing me to share their amazing grandmothers with the world.

My children, Gabriel, Emily, Dylan, Connor, and Owen, for making everything worthwhile.

My darling Thomas E. In a world where nothing is perfect, you are perfect for me.

To God. All glory and honor is Yours.

Grateful acknowledgments are made to the following for the permission to use their material:

Zella Spiers for "Vivid Images of a Summer Visit" (first appeared in *The Goochland Gazette*, summer 1993) and "Grandchildren Spark Memories of Summers Long Ago" (first appeared in *The Goochland Gazette*, late spring 1994).

Jeanie Kezo for "My Babcia."

Gabriel Ricard for "In a Perfect World."

Rosalie Franklin for "In My Nana's World."

Steven Sharp for "My Grandmother—My Teacher."

Krys Douglas for "The Legacy."

Brandy Blythe for "Learning to Say Goodbye."

Jennifer Blythe for "Remembering Granny."

LaRose Karr for "The Roses."

Wayne Scheer for "Communicating Love."

Peggy Duffy for "My One and Only Grandmother."

Contents

Preface

The Language of Flowers

Today's world contains no shortage of ways to communicate. We can send an e-mail across the globe in seconds and receive a response only moments later. Cell phones have become an essential accessory and people using them are a common sight in all but a few places.

Despite these sophisticated advances in communication technology, perhaps the most effective means of conveying our thoughts and feelings remain the most simple. A heartfelt note, the touch of a hand, or even a brilliant smile speaks volumes and carries meaningful messages long remembered.

Flowers have long been used to communicate a multitude of messages. We use flowers to congratulate, console, and commiserate. A bouquet can express feelings ranging from fond friendship to romantic love. Flowers have always had a language of their own, but it was during the reign of Queen Victoria that each bloom was given a unique meaning. The rose, once simply a symbol for romance, now carried a multitude of meanings with each color and variety possessing its own significance.

Using this unique and lovely language, we have created a special bouquet for a very special lady—Grandmother. With remarkable qualities in abundance, selecting only eight flowers for her bouquet proved to be no easy task. We could gather a garden of blossoms for this extraordinary lady and still be left searching for a way to tell her how much she means to us.

Chapter One

A Camellia for Admiration

Early western travelers to China and Japan fell in love with the exotic camellia, but their first attempts to cultivate this impressive beauty failed. Worried about the camellia's ability to adapt to a colder climate, enthusiasts pampered the plants in greenhouses. They didn't realize that, like our beloved grandmothers, these shrubs were not only beautiful but also vigorous and strong.

Gardeners have long admired the camellia for its hardiness, for its glossy evergreen leaves, and for the spectacular blossoms that can appear from late winter to early spring, announcing the long-awaited end to the drabness of winter. And so we admire our grandmothers for the color, strength, and beauty they bring to our lives.

Admiration

When we were young, we thought our grandmothers were amazing. A grandmother was, from our adoring perspective, a magician, capable of performing marvelous feats, a seer with the ability to answer our most difficult questions, and someone who made us feel like the most important person in the world. Long after we could make our own peanut butter and jam sandwiches, we longed for the ones she made. The four perfect triangles she served on our favorite plate were infinitely preferable to the oozing, slightly flattened concoction we came up with. And long after we could read, we begged our grandmothers for stories. They told us astonishing and true tales of long ago when our mother or father was a child—a concept we could scarcely imagine.

As the years passed, we learned things about our grandmothers that strengthened our deep admiration, but these discoveries only served to confirm what we realized at a very young age. No one ever had to tell us that Grandma was an extraordinary woman. We knew it, just as we knew that she loved us. And no matter how many wonderful, exotic meals we enjoyed, we would never forget how good those sandwiches tasted.

Better than a Fairytale

In the world of photography, it is highly unlikely that anyone would recognize the name of the man who took the picture. The frame I chose is not particularly valuable, but the photograph is priceless. It hangs on my living room wall and shows a beautiful young woman standing with one hand on the shoulder of the man beside her. At first you might think they are both standing, but upon closer inspection you realize that the man is seated. The tiny, almost doll-like woman was my paternal grandmother, and the big, broad-shouldered man was my grandfather. The photo was taken on their wedding day in 1914 when my grandmother, Maidie, was only sixteen years old. Her new husband, Robert, was forty-two.

Maidie was the youngest of four children, born late in her parents' lives. She was affectionately tolerated by her older sisters, teased mercilessly by her big brother, and cherished by her mother and father. After an unsuccessful attempt at homesteading on the Alberta prairie, her parents settled in the thriving city of Edmonton, Alberta, Canada, where they sometimes took in boarders to help pay the bills. One of these boarders was my grandfather, and when he and Maidie fell in love, her parents—most especially her mother—did little to encourage the romance.

As a young girl, this story fired my imagination more than most tales of fiction. I would look at my grandmother, then in her late sixties and early seventies, and search for evidence of the lovestruck teenager who married a man old enough to be her father. How did she convince her parents to consent? Did she threaten to run away? As much as I wanted to know, I couldn't bring myself to ask my grandmother. Although loving and kind, she was a private sort of person. So despite my intense curiosity, I chose to remain silent and let my mind fill in the blanks.

After thirty-six years of marriage, my grandfather died in 1952, three years before I was born. My father, quiet and reserved like my grandmother, didn't talk a lot about his childhood—certainly not enough to satisfy my voracious appetite for family stories—so my grandfather remained a stranger to me. I was lucky enough to have my grandmother in my life until 1986, when she died at the age of eighty-eight. I was witness to many events in her remarkable life, including her twenty-fifth wedding anniversary with her second husband, Jack, but I still wondered about the years she spent with my grandfather.

My grandparents had three children, James, Helen, and my father, Robert. My Aunt Helen had always been a special part of my life, but it wasn't until several years ago that I discovered she shared my passion for talking about the past and the people in it. I interrogated her with the zeal of a detective closing in on a suspect, and we often talked for hours. Her vivid recollections brought the past to life and gave me a renewed sense of my own identity. I loved hearing about the people who came before me—the people whose blood ran in my veins and whose very existence made my life possible.

Of course, I had to ask Aunt Helen about my grandmother and grandfather. "Was Grandma really only sixteen?" I asked. "And Grandpa was forty-two?"

"Yes, and her parents weren't very pleased about it," Aunt Helen replied.

"So what happened? Did Grandma threaten to run away? Was she defiant?"

"Oh, no, I don't think so," Aunt Helen said, and my heart sank. I had always been rather fond of my fantasy in which my rebellious young grandmother stands firm in her resolve to marry the man she loved.

"So how did she convince her parents to change their minds?" I asked.

Aunt Helen paused for a moment. "Well, I think, like most parents, they wanted her to be happy. And your grandfather made her happy. Very happy."

I smiled. The mental picture of my grandmother as a joyful young bride was far more satisfying than the one of her in active revolt against her parents' wishes. "And they were happy together?" I asked.

It was Aunt Helen's turn to smile. "Oh, yes. I remember your grandfather coming in after a long, hard day. Your grandmother was usually in the kitchen, and he would stop to give her a kiss before he did anything else. I don't recall him being anything but gentle and kind with her, and she adored him."

As much as I relished the thought of my grandmother being adored, I hated the idea of her being widowed when she was only fifty-three. "Grandpa died of a heart attack, didn't he?" I asked Aunt Helen one day.

"Yes," she said. "He and your grandmother had spent the evening visiting with friends. Your grandmother made one of her coconut cream pies—you remember her pies, don't you?"

"Of course I do," I replied, and our conversation took a sharp turn to the subject of my grandmother's baking. I recalled my father telling me that he and his best friend would come home from school and eat half a pie each. Dinner at my grandmother's meant a choice of desserts, usually including several different kinds of pie, and there was always fresh bread and dinner rolls.

"Your grandfather ate a quarter of a pie that night," Aunt Helen said, continuing our previous discussion, "and as soon as he and your grandmother got home, he had a hot bath and went to bed. When your grandmother went upstairs later, he was dead."

Overwhelmed by an abrupt feeling of sadness, I thought of my grandmother climbing the stairs to bed, tired but contented after an evening with friends. Maybe she was thinking of my grandfather eating a slice of his favorite pie, and then holding up his plate for seconds and telling her it was the best pie she had ever made. She went into the bedroom, moving in that quiet way she had, so as not to disturb him. And then she made her heart-breaking discovery.

At first I found myself wishing that she hadn't been by herself that night. Later, though, I saw her in my mind, sitting on the bed beside him. She knew she would have to call the family in a few minutes, but that could wait until she said good-bye to the man who had loved and cherished her for thirty-six years. She may have been facing the rest of her life without him, but for those last few moments, they were still together.

A grandmother is a little bit parent, a little bit teacher, and a little bit best friend.

—Author Unknown

My Babcia

I was only about twelve when my grandmother died. That was many years ago, and even though I now have grandchildren of my own, I know my grandmother lives on in my traditions, my work ethic, and the love I have for my family.

My grandparents emigrated from Poland several years before I was born. They settled in Two Rivers, Wisconsin, and lived in a house with a white picket fence and a majestic cherry tree in the backyard. My parents and I lived upstairs in the same house, an arrangement that found me spending more time downstairs than up.

Despite their move to America, my grandparents still preferred to converse in their native tongue and, inevitably, I picked up some of the language. From my little girl's perspective, speaking Polish seemed as normal as speaking English, and I recall thinking that all children were bilingual. I loved listening to them speak Polish. The soft consonants and rolling "r's" soothed me like a lullaby.

The holidays highlighted my grandparents' Polish heritage in special ways. Every Thanksgiving, Grandma prepared a roast turkey that was expertly stuffed with sausage and sage and basted with sautéed onions and butter. Before we exchanged gifts on Christmas Eve, she hosted a Polish Catholic meal that included baked ham with all the trimmings, blessed Communion wafers, and pickled herring. The day before Easter, she boiled eggs in a stew of red onion peelings, a natural food coloring that I never saw anyone else use. It always amazed me to see the eggshells turn brick red.

Traditions like these found their true significance years later when I adopted them for my own family. As a child, however, it didn't matter if my grandmother spoke a different language or cooked unusual foods. I only know that I loved to spend time with her because I knew she cared about me and made me feel special. I remember those days with great fondness.

Grandma included me in her numerous activities and she never made me feel like an annoyance or a distraction. I was her cherished assistant and helped her guide clothes through a wringer washer and, later, watched her iron them under a mangle iron. She retrained my left-handedness into right and sometimes permed my hair into a wild Brillo pad. When I was sick, she took care of me.

As time passed, I realized that Grandma possessed strengths shared by grandmothers of many cultures. Grandpa may have been the soul of our family, but Grandma was its muscle. Hardworking and unselfish, she dedicated herself to her family and her home. She made her own cheese, soups, and pressure-cooked meals that sometimes exploded and stuck to the ceiling. She grew fresh vegetables in a rented garden plot, and sometimes we searched for edible mushrooms in the nearby woods.

When she died, I could not believe how my world changed, and I will never forget the depth of my sadness. The years have softened the pain of her passing, but her essence and the lessons she taught me will always remain.

Jeanie Kezo

It is as grandmothers that our mothers
come into the fullness of their grace.

—Christopher Morley

The Feeling Is Mutual

My mother-in-law, Mildred, welcomed my children and me into the family with her words but, more importantly, she received us with her heart. She was a mother of ten and grandmother of nineteen, and one might think her love had been stretched to the limit, but a heart like hers had no boundaries. She had love enough for everyone and an endless supply in reserve.

With the ease of someone slipping into a coat, she became the grandmother my children needed and wanted. When the cards arrived for each and every birthday, when I saw the children's artwork displayed on her fridge, and when I watched her surrounded by family, her face softened with love, I decided that, as far as grandmothers were concerned, my children had hit the jackpot. They had been gifted with a grandmother whose presence and influence would bless the rest of their lives.

My admiration for Mildred began when I discovered that my husband was one of ten children. My four children regularly depleted my time and patience—I couldn't imagine adding six to the equation without forfeiting a good portion of my sanity. My respect for Mom, as she asked me to call her, blossomed when I met her other children. They were, without exception, genuine, decent people and a credit to their remarkable mother.

So many times, I longed to come right out and ask her, "How did you do it? Where did you find the endurance and understanding? How did you find the strength to go on when your son was killed and when you lost a granddaughter and grandson in tragic accidents? How did you say good-bye to your husband of over fifty years and learn to live alone?"

The answers to these questions came when I took the time to get to know her better. I discovered that Mom took each day as it came, believing that God would never give her more than she could handle. Her powerful faith inspired me to increase my own reliance on God and, in turn, encourage my children to do so. They loved Grandma Millie for remembering their birthdays, for making the special treats they enjoyed, and for the hugs that always made them feel special. I knew that, in the years to come, they would also love her for teaching them what was really important.

One morning Mom phoned and, in the course of the conversation, I decided to tell her how much I admired her. I did my best to explain why I felt the way I did, and when I was finished, there was a brief silence. When she finally responded, I could tell my words had moved her. "Thank you," she said. "I don't think I've ever done anything all that extraordinary. Truth is, I've always admired you. You have such wonderful children, and you've done such a good job raising them."

Her words came as a complete surprise, and it was my turn to be rendered speechless. No gift, wrapped in elegant paper and decorated with a red satin bow, would have been as welcome or valuable as the tribute she paid me that day. The day my children hit the jackpot, I did, too.

She is more precious than rubies: and all the things thou canst desire are not to be compared unto her. Length of days is in her right hand; and in her left hand riches and honor. Her ways are ways of pleasantness, and all her paths are peace.

—Proverbs 3:15–17

Chapter Two

A Dandelion for Happiness and Wishes Come True

Just as happiness can bloom in the midst of cold, dark times in our lives, the dandelion's bright yellow flowers appear in early spring, no matter how cool the weather may be. Some may question the inclusion of what may be considered a weed and a pest in our grandmother's bouquet, but the cheerful yellow dandelion and its promise of spring is like a sunny smile abruptly appearing on a solemn face.

Overnight, the yellow flower changes to a white seed head. Hundreds of seeds, each one with its own tiny parachute, stand ready to travel where the wind takes them. As long as there have been dandelions, there have been children to pick them, make a fervent wish, and blow on the white cluster to start the tiny seeds on their journey. Some of us may still pick our own dandelion, if only to pause and remember a time when we believed that wishes come true.

We've chosen the dandelion to represent the happiness our grandmothers bring—a feeling of joy that, like the tiny seeds, knows no distance and, like the bright spring flowers, brings endless smiles. Just watch a grandmother roller-skating with her grandson or reading to her granddaughter, and you will realize that the happiness is far from one-sided. As for wishes and whether or not they come true, you only have to ask the grandmother holding her newborn grandchild.

Happiness and Wishes Come True

As mothers we faced exhaustion, frustration, and days that seemed to never end. We changed diapers, played tooth fairy, and read favorite stories so many times that we were able to recite them in our sleep. We struggled through the first day of kindergarten, the first sleepover, and the first date. We fought wars over music, curfews, and piercings.

Then, without warning, we found ourselves deafened by the silence of an empty house. When did the little girl surrounded by dolls become the young woman in a white dress pledging her love to her new husband? When did the little boy with a face covered with dirt and jam turn into the young man in a tuxedo dedicating his life to his new bride?

But, as many of us discovered, what appeared to be an ending was, in fact, only a beginning. The announcement that we were going to be grandmothers took some of us by surprise. For others, it brought the fulfillment of our heart's desire, and the happiness we clung to in our memories found new life as we pictured our floors once more cluttered with toys, and heard our rooms echo with the sound of a child's voice.

When Dreams Come True

The pastor of our church, Ted, and his wife, Anne, have two grown daughters. Dawn and Angela, both happily married, are bright, attractive, and very accomplished women in their thirties. Whenever Anne talks about her girls, I hear an abundance of love and pride in her voice, but until recently I also detected a slightly wistful note when the subject of grandchildren came up. It was more than obvious to me that she deeply wanted to be a grandmother.

We all rejoiced with Dawn and her husband, Clifton, when they announced that Dawn was expecting a baby. Although they were only occasional visitors to our church, I had come to care for Dawn very much, and I was thrilled that she was going to be a mother. I think Anne may have been more excited than anyone, with the exception—perhaps—of Dawn and Clifton.

A few weeks after the exciting announcement, however, Dawn suffered a miscarriage. Just as we had celebrated with her and Clifton earlier, we now grieved with them. I, too, had suffered a miscarriage, and I had a pretty good idea of how devastated Dawn and Clifton must be. And even though Anne didn't say much, I knew she shared their heartbreak.

It has been said that God does not close a door without opening another. Within a few months, Dawn was pregnant for the second time. Cautious excitement filled the air, and Dawn was understandably nervous. When Anne announced that Dawn was having terrible morning sickness, I told her it was a very good sign. "I'm sorry she's having a rough time," I said, "but strong symptoms mean her hormones are doing their job, and those are the hormones that keep her pregnancy going."

Anne's grateful smile told me that my words were providing her with much-needed encouragement. And when she came to church with the news that Dawn's first ultrasound had shown a baby with a strong and steady heartbeat, I was able to provide additional words of support. "Once a heartbeat is detected," I said, "the chances of miscarriage are almost nonexistent."

I don't think anyone ever completely relaxed when it came to Dawn's pregnancy. The specter of her earlier experience was difficult to banish, but as her stomach swelled, so did our confidence. Several ultrasounds confirmed that Dawn's pregnancy was progressing normally. Anne faithfully reported the results of these ultrasounds, and we followed the news with the avid interest and concern of any family waiting for a new member to arrive.

When it was discovered during one of the ultrasounds that the baby was a girl, Anne's cup of happiness overflowed. She walked around with a look on her face that suggested she and Ted had just won Virginia's biggest lottery. We soon learned that Dawn and Clifton had chosen the name Ava for their precious girl, and it wasn't long before Anne found herself unable to resist the lure of impossibly tiny shoes and little pink clothes. "I found the cutest outfits for Ava, and they were all on sale," she told us, one Sunday, while Ted, standing behind her, rolled his eyes in mock exasperation.

Prayers of thanksgiving were plentiful the day Ava finally arrived. A healthy baby is always a cause for celebration, but for Dawn and Clifton, the fleeting memories of their earlier sorrow made their joy much sweeter and their gratitude more heartfelt. Anne returned from her first visit to the hospital with photographic evidence that her granddaughter was the most beautiful baby in the world.

Understandably, Ava became Anne's favorite subject. Anne may have waited a long time to become a grandmother, but she wasn't going to waste a minute enjoying her new role. There was no doubt in my mind that the day Ava came into the world was the day that one of Anne's dreams came true.

Anne leads a women's Bible study every Sunday morning. We sit around the big table in the church kitchen for an hour while she presents informative and helpful lessons based on the Bible. Sometimes, though, we just sit and visit. These are special times for me as I learn more about the members of my church family. One day, some months after Ava's birth, the topic turned to babies, and Dawn's miscarriage was mentioned.

Anne grew very quiet. Then she stepped out of her role as the pastor's wife and our teacher, and became any woman whose life had been touched by sadness. She told us that Dawn's loss had been hard to bear, not only because her dream of having a grandchild was left unrealized, but also because she had to watch her own child suffer and grieve. "For a long time," she said, "I found it hard to get excited about other people's babies or even walk through the baby department at the store. Not just because it made me sad, but because I couldn't help but think about how badly Dawn must be feeling."

No one said anything for a few minutes. We were all mothers, and I don't think there was a woman at the table who didn't understand what Anne was trying to say. Finally I pointed to the framed photo of newborn Ava on the table in front of me. "But now Clifton and Dawn have Ava," I said.

Anne grinned. "And I have the most gorgeous granddaughter in the world."

And because all babies have their own miraculous beauty, everyone quickly agreed that Ava was an exceedingly lovely child. "She makes me so happy," Anne said. "And part of that happiness comes from knowing how much joy she's brought into my daughter's life." She paused and cocked her head slightly as if thinking about what she had just said. "Does that make sense?" she asked.

"Perfect sense," I said.

If I had known how wonderful it would be to have grandchildren, I'd have had them first.

—Lois Wyse

Vivid Images of a Summer Visit

During summers long ago, we would descend upon my husband's home place with five tots and an appalling collection of nursery equipment. We were usually joined by my husband's siblings with many small offspring of their own. I can still see my father-in-law, on the day of our departure, sprawled in his recliner. Eyes twinkling, he would say, "You all have made me twice glad—glad to see you come and glad to see you go."

Our realistic friends joked that we might have the same feeling once the summer visits of our own grandchildren ended. It's true that their departure was followed by a driving need on my part for more afternoon naps, but it's also true that our granddaughters left behind vivid and unforgettable images to refresh us long after their visit was over.

Since this was their first visit to our farmhouse, I had to warn them about the troublesome hearth brick that sat waiting to snag unsuspecting toes—especially bare ones. "Mind the brick" became a much-repeat caution. The children—Lydia, aged seven, Bobbie, aged five, and Taylor, twenty-two months—turned the phrase into a litany, soon reminding everyone to "mind the brick."

One afternoon I heard Bobbie muttering to herself. "Mind the brick, mind the step, mind the stairs, and mind the Grandma," she said. "There sure are lots of things to mind around here." But then she came and hugged my knees. "I like it here, Grandma. Can we come again next summer?" she asked.

We took the two older girls to the pony futurity at Deep Run. They sat primly, side by side, on lawn chairs under a tree. Ponies and handlers, waiting to enter the ring, had also sought shade. I overheard Lydia warning her sister. "Don't move, Bobbie," she said. "We're surrounded by ponies!"

Later, a kindly local breeder invited the girls to pat her handsome gray colt. The girls were enthralled, and our next visit to the library revealed a new interest in books about ponies. When reading the books, the girls insisted we change the names of human characters to Lydia and Bobbie.

Grandma began to dream about a pony in the pasture by next summer. Granddaddy began to look anxious.

Our smallest granddaughter, Taylor, was accompanied by her parents, but she awakened earlier than they did most mornings. She immediately searched for the Old Fellow, eager to snap on his leash and take him for a walk. She trudged a quarter mile on her small but sturdy legs, her Pampers creating a jaunty, swinging stride. She wore a small baseball cap, always with the bill turned backward. Her determined goal was a neighbor's pasture where a horse and pony grazed, and she held her small palm flat, as she had been instructed, so they could eat from her hand. Her toothy grin and her whispered "Soft" also remain with us.

Old Fellow had belonged to the girls' parents when they were younger and hadn't been in the company of little ones for a long time. He welcomed them with all the enthusiasm a dog nearing sixteen could manage, and the children, sensing his fragility, treated him with respectful affection. Even the ginger cats were won over. The girls heeded my warning not to chase them and practiced restraint. Soon, they were rewarded by arched backs rubbing their legs and by purring heard easily on the tranquil hillside.

At first, Lydia was a bit awed by the silence of country life. One night she came downstairs and explained why she couldn't sleep. "I hear the quiet."

They have all gone back to Texas now. I think of them each time I make my way around the brick. I think of all the bricks that may wait along their pathways in a troubled world. Their small faces swim before me. I whisper, "Mind the bricks" and "Twice glad," and dream of next summer's visit.

Zella Spiers

"Few things are more delightful than grandchildren fighting over your lap."

—Doug Larson

The Roses

Becoming grandparents didn't happen with us in the usual way. We didn't go to the hospital nursery and gaze at a sleepy newborn through a window. Grandparenting came to us in a big way when our son married a woman with four children!

At first we were thrilled because our son was thrilled, but we soon discovered the delight in having little ones in our life again. Many years had passed since we tickled children, or wrestled with them on the floor, but we quickly remembered how sweet it is to have them climb into your lap, or shout your name when they see you.

My youngest granddaughter cannot say my name so she calls me "The Roses," and I have become "The Roses" to my friends as well. There are no moments more precious than the ones spent with children. I loved every moment of being a mom, and now I cherish every moment spent with my newly acquired grandchildren.

Once again, toys adorn my home. Crayons, coloring books, and dollies rest in a cradle near the front door. The toy box has been put back in its old spot. And, with the return of sweet kisses and hugs from children, our season for grandparenting has begun!

LaRose Karr

She is a tree of life to them that lay hold upon her: and happy is every one that retaineth her.

—Proverbs 3:18

Strength and honor are her clothing; and she shall rejoice in time to come.

—Proverbs 31:25

Chapter Three

A Honeysuckle for Generous and Devoted Affection

The plentiful honeysuckle flower is a perfect choice to symbolize the generous and devoted affection of our grandmothers. The rambling honeysuckle vine, blanketed with a profusion of long, tubular red blooms, is a welcome addition to any garden. Its fragrant blooms create a haven for ruby-throated hummingbirds, honeybees, and butterflies—lovely creatures that will fill your garden with the sounds and sights of summer.

The honeysuckle is easily propagated and just as easily maintained. The vines are winter-hardy, heat-tolerant, and nearly indestructible. They bring to mind our grandmothers' abundant affection that, once rooted, is faithful and true—and, most certainly, enduring.

Generous and Devoted Affection

When asked to describe our grandmother, some of us might relate details of her physical appearance and smile when we say, "I look just like her." Others might talk about their grandmother's penchant for yard sales, or the weekly column she writes for the local paper. And if our grandmother is gone, we might recall the little things we've come to remember in the years since her death—the fact that she loved the color blue and couldn't quote *Charlotte's Web* without crying. We might even name the perfume she used to wear.

No description of our grandmothers would be complete without mentioning her abundant and unconditional love. She loves us just the way we are. She loves us no matter what, and when we feel like our world has turned dark and cold, she lights our way and warms us with a love that is never in short supply.

A Grandmother for Dylan

When I married Tom, I had four young children, three of whom had never known my mother, their only grandmother. My logical side knew that grandmothers were not a prerequisite to a happy childhood. Neither were grandfathers, aunts, uncles, and cousins. But my emotional side recalled the joys of having a large and loving extended family, and I longed for my children to know that happiness, too.

Tom was one of ten children. His parents were both living, and he had eleven nieces and nephews. Everyone welcomed us into the family, and I rejoiced that my children would finally enjoy the experiences I remembered so fondly. Some of Tom's brothers and sisters were spread across the country, but his parents and two of his sisters lived about a two-hour drive from our home. We got together for special occasions such as Thanksgiving and Christmas, and the children grew to love Grandma Millie as if she'd been their grandmother since they were born. She remembered every birthday and special event, subscribed to magazines she didn't need, and proudly displayed their artwork on her fridge.

When Owen was born, we became a family of seven. We also became a family looking for a larger house. Our search led us deeper and deeper into the country where real estate was less expensive, and where we could find the extra land we had always wanted. We fell in love with a big, old farmhouse with several acres, and within a few months, we had moved in. Unfortunately, we now lived farther away from Tom's mother and sisters, and family gatherings became less frequent. Although delighted with our new home, I was saddened by the thought that my children wouldn't be spending very much time with their new family.

A few years later, Tom suffered a near-fatal accident. He confessed to me weeks later that, while he was in the hospital recovering, he had made a promise to God that if he survived, he would begin taking his family to church. Neither one of us had been to church for years, and we had no idea how to go about finding one to attend.

Then, one spring day, two men stopped by the farm and invited us to attend Sussex Baptist Church, about ten miles down the road. Father's Day was approaching, and I asked Tom what he would like. "I'd like you to come to church with me on Father's Day," he said. I was less than enthusiastic, but persuaded by a strong feeling that I should honor his request, I agreed to go. It was one of the best decisions I have ever made.

The few churches I had attended over the years had been massive, cathedral-type buildings filled with strangers. When the service was over, I knew no more about the person sitting next to me than I had when it started. Being rather shy by nature, I found myself hoping that the church I had promised to visit would offer me the anonymity I had experienced in other churches.

When I walked in the door on Father's Day morning, I saw small groups of people of varying ages and dressed in all manner of attire. They were talking, smiling, and exchanging handshakes and hugs. They appeared to actually like each other. What I didn't know, yet, was that these people and their actions were genuine.

Their behavior made me feel both unsettled and wistful at the same time. Before I could give it any more thought, however, a woman who I later discovered was the pastor's wife, Anne, hurried over to greet us. After we introduced ourselves, she took us on a quick tour and made sure we met every single person along the way. I left that day still a bit unnerved, but perfectly willing to return. I had a feeling that these kind and sincere people had something I wanted.

It wasn't long before I discovered what made the members of this church unique. I heard the people around me using the term "church family," and after a few weeks of getting to know them, I realized that they saw their congregation as a large extended family. Like all families, there were good times and bad, disagreements and reconciliation, but in times of sorrow and hardship, or if anyone needed help of any kind, they came together as a family and did whatever needed to be done.

In addition to Sunday morning services, we also went to church Wednesday evenings. The adults met for Bible study in the sanctuary while the children enjoyed games and snacks next door in the large school building. I loved watching the children, ranging in age from toddlers to teenagers, playing together. I smiled at the sight of the older children helping the younger ones and cheering them on. The scene reminded me of the family gatherings long ago on my aunt and uncle's farm. After an enormous potluck supper, my cousins and I would play games such as baseball and hide-and-seek in the gathering dusk, while our parents watched us from lawn chairs spread around the yard.

In the months that followed, we grew to care deeply for our new extended family. I was drawn, in particular, to a motherly woman in her seventies, affectionately known as Miss Helen. She gave me a sense of well-being and security that made me think of my mother. As we spent more time together, enjoying our common interests such as reading and gardening, I realized how much I missed having someone to guide and nurture me.

One Sunday Miss Helen asked me if she could borrow my teenage son, Dylan, to help her with some yard work. She picked

Dylan up the next morning; when he returned that evening, he was smiling and full of stories about his day. Over the next year, Dylan would often spend his Saturdays with Miss Helen and her husband, Yancy. They usually gave Dylan ten dollars. One day, he told me that he didn't feel right about taking the money. "I like helping them," he said.

"I know you do," I replied, "but giving you the money makes Miss Helen and Yancy feel better about asking you to help them and taking up your time."

"I would do it for nothing," he said. "I love Miss Helen. I wish she was my grandma."

I told Dylan that Miss Helen made me feel like I had a mother again. "You don't have to be related to someone for them to be a part of your family," I said. "There's absolutely no reason she can't be your grandma. I guess you could say she's your grandma of the heart."

Dylan nodded. "I like that," he said. "So, do you think it's okay if I call her Grandma?"

"Oh," I said with a slight catch in my voice, "I think that would be more than okay. I think it would be wonderful."

Grandmother-grandchildren relationships are simple. Grandmas are short on criticism and long on love.

—Author Unknown

Communicating Love

My grandmother's English was about equal to my four-year-old command of the language. And, just to confuse me further, she would add strange-sounding Yiddish and Polish words. Still, she had no trouble communicating her love for me, her first grandchild. She sang, and she cooked. What more could any child ask for?

When I think of visiting my grandmother, what I remember most was sitting on her lap in an oversized rocking chair, rocking to the rhythm of her singing. The songs were in languages I didn't understand, but it didn't matter. Her voice was soft and soothing, like the shawl she'd drape over my shoulders. Sometimes I'd nap as she sang, and sometimes she'd tickle me at appropriate points in her medley, and we'd giggle like two children. In my mind she was both childlike and maternal, offering both friendship and security to a young boy who was often the only child present when the family gathered. My sister would be born later, as well as cousins, but she and I still found rocking-chair time.

Then there was the food. Always a strange combination of the exotic and familiar. Huge mounds of kasha varnishkes with a giant meatball on top, roasted chicken, brisket and mashed potatoes. I never had to eat vegetables when she cooked—meats and starches filled her table. And beets. How could I forget the beets? Blood red to purple, slimy and foul, they were sometimes submerged in what smelled like soured milk. She'd laugh at the face I'd make and say, "No like, boychic? No eat." Thankfully, my parents never made me even taste the beets. In fact, as I recall, they'd take only small amounts for themselves.

Dinner always ended with freshly baked cookies. Simple globs of dough covered with sugar. There'd be cakes and pies the relatives brought from local bakeries, but Grandma's cookies were far more satisfying.

As an adult, I regret that I never had a conversation with my grandmother that I can remember. In her later years, she developed Alzheimer's and spoke only in a language that even the old-timers couldn't understand. But I recall bringing my toddler son to see her at the very end of her life. She had grown bedridden and nonresponsive. But when she saw him, she managed to squeeze herself out of bed and play ring-around-the rosy with him. Afterwards, she sat on the rocker in her room, with him on her lap, singing, and tickling him.

I can still hear them giggling.

She still knew how to communicate.

Wayne Scheer

A garden of love grows in a grandmother's heart.

—Author Unknown

The Package Deal

You might say Tom got a package deal. When he became my husband on November 20, 1998, he also became my four children's stepfather. Gabriel, Emily, Dylan, and Connor had been the biggest part of my life since before their births, and I adored them, but Tom was new to the roller-coaster ride known as parenting, and I worried that it might be a bit overwhelming.

Like a baby learning to walk, the six of us took our first hesitant steps toward building a life together. And because we were only human, we faltered and sometimes fell. With a little time and lots of love, the bruised feelings and scraped egos healed, and we carried on, our confidence growing with every step. When Owen arrived, he blessed us all and gave us a powerful sense of purpose. It took a tiny baby to make it official—we were a real family.

Tom may have been a novice parent, but his mother was most definitely a veteran. She was a mother to ten and a grandmother to eleven when my children and I arrived on the scene. As the younger of two children, I could hardly imagine what life had been like for Tom, growing up with nine siblings. I loved hearing about his family, but when the invitation to a family Thanksgiving dinner arrived, I was the one who felt overwhelmed.

Would they like me? Would I feel welcome? More importantly, would the children feel welcome? Despite a chronic case of shyness that had plagued me since childhood, I knew I could make it through the dinner, but the mother bear in me hesitated to take my babies into uncharted emotional territory.

I will always remember the first time I saw Tom's mother, Mildred. Dinner was being held at the home of Tom's sister Janet, and upon our arrival, we found ourselves surrounded by numerous members of his family. Once again, I had worried needlessly. Everyone was exceedingly kind. They also seemed remarkably tall. I am just a little over five feet tall, and I recall feeling very short during those first few moments. Amid the noise and confusion, I managed to hear Tom say, "I'd like you to meet my mom." And there she was, her warm and generous smile adding volumes to her words of welcome. My sense of relief increased when I realized that, unlike everyone else in attendance, she wasn't looking down at me. Our eyes met, and I gratefully returned her smile.

That afternoon, Mildred made it abundantly clear that when Tom became my children's father, she became their grandmother. She fussed over the new baby as any proud grandmother would, but not once did she exclude the other children from her attentions or affection.

When the time came to go home, we gathered at the front door to say our good-byes. Four-year-old Connor tugged at my sleeve and, when I bent down, he pointed to Tom's mom. "Is she our grandma?" he said. Embarrassed by his candor, I flushed and nodded. Obviously satisfied with my answer, he waved and grinned. "Good-bye, Grandma!" he announced in a much louder voice.

Mildred's eager wave and big smile told me my response to Connor's question had pleased her, too. "Good-bye, Connor," she said. That was the day I found a grandmother for my children. That was also the day I found out how easy it was to love her.

For though I be absent in the flesh,
yet am I with you in the spirit, joying
and beholding your order, and the
steadfastness of your faith in Christ.

—Colossians 2:5

Chapter Four

A Myrtle for Love in Absence

The true myrtle, or *Myrtus communis,* is a dense evergreen shrub, generally recognized for its glossy, pungent leaves and medicinal uses. Like tiny sparklers on the Fourth of July, the sweetly scented blooms, each with an amazing number of stamens, cover the bush each summer. Proving that beauty and function can be inseparable, the myrtle flower does not fade and die, but is transformed into an edible blue berry.

We've chosen the dainty myrtle flower to symbolize a love that defies separation. Distance and circumstance may prevent a grandmother from seeing her beloved grandchildren, but nothing can diminish her deep attachment to them. Hearts and minds remain united across continents, oceans, and the occasions that sometimes force us apart.

Love in Absence

Few of us can define love, but we've all experienced it and readily acknowledge its power. It's a life-changing, complicated, and sometimes painful emotion. The Greeks knew love wasn't easily explained. In an effort to describe the different types of love we humans encounter, they used not one but four words. They realized that a mother's love for her child was not the same as the love she had for her husband, her friends, or her God.

All these forms of love, however, have a great deal in common. When we love, we are most alive. Love is our precious legacy from God, and the greatest gift we can bestow. Like a tenacious weed, it will take root and grow, even in adverse conditions, and efforts to destroy it are often in vain. And just as a weed will survive under circumstances that destroy an entire garden, our love endures, and may even flourish, through life's most difficult moments.

Becoming a Grandmother

I don't ever recall my mother expressing a longing to become a grandmother. My brother and I both got married in our twenties, but my mother never once hinted at the possibility of grandchildren. My brother's wife had a son, Craig, from a previous marriage. Craig had no shortage of grandmothers, great-grandmothers, grandfathers, and great-grandfathers, so when the time came to decide what Craig would call my parents, my mother suggested that, to avoid confusion, Craig could use her and my father's first names—Bob and Barbara. I teased my mother, telling her that she made the suggestion to avoid being called "Grandmother." If I remember correctly, she didn't find my comment particularly funny.

I was twenty-nine when I announced my first pregnancy. Both my parents were distinctly ambivalent. They didn't convey any disapproval, but they weren't overly excited, either. Their reaction didn't surprise or upset me—it was pretty much in character for them. But because they knew it was something that I wanted very much, they were supportive and encouraging. As with other significant experiences in my life up to that point, I knew they would be there to help me should I need it.

A few months after my announcement, my husband and I moved to another town. Home became a small cabin on the outskirts of a remote logging community. We were unable to get television reception, and my only companions during the day were the radio and my dog, Sadie. I didn't mind because all my previous interests had vanished, replaced by an obsession with my expanding abdomen and the still unnamed resident within. I brought stacks of pregnancy books home from the tiny town library and made lengthy lists of baby names and even longer lists of every possible thing that my baby might need—for the next twenty years.

I talked to my mother on the phone every day. I would often read her my current list of things, and she would add her latest choices. She loved discussing names, but when I brought up my list of baby supplies, she was less than enthusiastic. "You have lots of time to get things for the baby," she said. I confess I was a bit hurt, especially since my mother's passion for shopping was only eclipsed by her passion for her family. Maybe she was waiting for her favorite department store to have its annual baby sale. In any case, I was beginning to long for impossibly tiny baby clothes. I wanted to touch them, and fold them, and arrange them in a drawer. I had wanted my mother to share the experience with me, but, as she pointed out, there was still a lot of time. I wasn't going to give up hope.

By the time I saw my mother again, I was feeling most definitely pregnant and had developed a rather large tummy. My husband finally took a few days off, and we planned a visit to see my parents. When we pulled into their driveway, they came out to greet us. I stepped out of the truck, and my mother's eyes widened in surprise. "Well, look at you," she said with a smile. "I guess there is no doubt about it now."

I was still in the process of getting used to my new shape and felt quite awkward and more than a little self-conscious. Those feelings disappeared, however, when my mother hurried over and gave me a big hug. "You look wonderful. You haven't gained weight anywhere except here," she said and gently patted my stomach. Her words acted on me like a rain shower on the summer's hottest day, and, although I wasn't absolutely certain, I thought I detected a glitter of excitement in her eyes.

Inside the house, we talked about the baby. I told my parents that we hadn't decided on a name yet. "Well," my mother said. "I've decided that I want the baby to call me Grammy. Not Grandma, or Granny, or Nana, but Grammy."

I smiled at the thought of her giving such careful consideration to her new title but I decided not to tease her this time. Obviously this was important to her, so I simply said, "I think Grammy is a terrific name."

My mother excused herself from the table where we were having our cake and coffee. She returned a few minutes later, staggering under the weight of shopping bags and boxes. "I've done a little shopping," she said. "But I'm really waiting for Woodward's big baby sale. I think it's next month."

I grinned, and my father made a dramatic show of rolling his eyes. "I survived raising two children," he said, "but my first grandchild is going to bankrupt me." He tried to keep his voice serious, but my mother's feigned indignation and protests reduced him to laughter.

Unfortunately, not long after that visit, my husband's job forced us to move again, this time six hundred miles away. Although I was looking forward to living in a place I always had wanted to visit, I knew how much I would miss my mother. We parted with promises to call often. My mother had always loved writing book-length letters, so I knew we would be staying in touch by mail as well.

Getting settled in our new home kept me busy for the first few weeks after we arrived, but it wasn't long before I began to suffer from increasingly frequent bouts of homesickness. The countdown to the baby's due date was now being calculated in weeks rather than months, and I knew it wouldn't be long before we began to measure the time in days. The simple truth was that I wanted my mother. I needed more than her voice on the phone or her words in a letter. I wanted her to be there when the baby was born. I derived small comfort from the fact that she wanted this as much as I did. But neither one of us could change the fact that her failing health wouldn't allow her to make the trip.

About two weeks before the baby's due date, I began to experience some uncomfortable cramplike sensations. And with absolutely no idea as to what constituted labor, I went to the doctor. He confirmed that I had begun to dilate and suggested that I check into the local hospital. We hurried home to get my things and I stopped to call my mother. Trembling with nervous excitement, I told her that this was it. The baby was on his or her way.

That evening, I called her again, but not to announce the birth of her grandchild. After spending almost an entire day waiting for more contractions, the doctor had decided that I might as well go home. "First babies can be tricky," he said. "Your labor could start again tonight, or it could happen days from now." His words almost reduced me to tears. I had been so sure I would be leaving the hospital cradling a baby.

Now, on the phone, I could hear the disappointment in her voice. "I phoned all my friends," she said.

"You did?" I replied, my frustration momentarily forgotten. I loved the thought of her making those calls and sharing her anticipation.

Two weeks later, Gabriel made his appearance at eleven o'clock in the morning. At my first opportunity, I shuffled to the pay phone down the hall and dialed my parents' number. When no one answered the phone, I checked the time and realized that my father must be at work. My mother was undoubtedly out shopping somewhere. I'll try again in a few hours, I thought, and called some of my friends and relatives.

A few hours later, I called my parents again. This time, my mother answered, and I was finally able to say the words she—and everyone else—had been waiting to hear. In a description overflowing with clichés, I introduced her new grandson. "He's beautiful," I said. "He's perfect. He's got your hands."

I paused to hear her response, but there was only silence on the other end of the line. Then I heard a quiet sniffle, and I realized she was crying. Neither one of us said anything for a few moments. Finally, my mother spoke. "How soon can you come for a visit?" she asked.

"Soon," I said. "Very, very soon."

"I'm not sure I can wait," she said and sighed. I laughed and marveled at the love that already existed between my mother and Gabriel—a love that had begun to grow in spite of distance and absence, and one that would continue to thrive and blossom in the years that followed.

If your baby is beautiful and perfect, never cries or fusses, sleeps on schedule and burps on demand, an angel all the time, you're the grandma.

—Teresa Bloomingdale

The Legacy

My grandmother died when I was little more than two years old. Although I never had the opportunity to get to know her in person, I became well acquainted with her through what my grandfather and my mother said about her, and through letters she wrote to be given to me when I was older.

I was told that I was the center of her universe, and the smiles she wears in my baby pictures prove that I was, indeed, one of her greatest joys. It was the letters, however, that told me what kind of person she was and that revealed the dreams she had for me. Unfortunately, the precious letters no longer exist. The box that held them was taken during a burglary decades ago. It was a heartbreaking loss, but even though the thief took the letters, he couldn't steal the words from my heart—words I will never forget. In one letter she wrote, "Remember you are loved for who you are not what you do. Remember that and you can do anything."

She was born into a world where women had little or no voice and where they were expected to know their place in life. However, my grandmother had a keen business mind and defied tradition when she found her own place as the manager of my grandfather's construction business. She had a strong sense of social justice and, in 1916, she and a few other women in the farming community where she lived chained themselves to the fence around the county courthouse, protesting in favor of the right to vote.

This beautiful woman, with a smile that could light the world, left me a legacy in the form of letters full of love but, above all, filled with encouragement. These letters, along with the extraordinary example she set in her own life, taught me to be confident, to be kind, to be committed, and, most of all, to be my own woman.

Krys Douglas

*Grandmas hold our tiny hands for just
a little while, but our hearts forever.*

—Author Unknown

In a Perfect World

My grandmother died about two months after I turned three. I'm twenty-one now, and I realize that having her in my life, even for that brief period, was a gift—one that I see many people taking for granted. When I think of her, I can't help feeling a bit cheated, because I know I missed out on something really special. Apart from those few short years, I've been forced to rely on photographs and stories from other family members, and I can't help but wish that our time together had been longer.

One time, at my grandparents' house, I fell down a small flight of stairs. Feeling as though I had cracked my head open, I began to howl. Suddenly, she was right there, taking me into her arms, stroking the back of my head, and telling me that I was okay. I can't help but smile when I remember that my tears were short-lived that day, especially after she gave me a small toy.

Of course, I didn't know it then, but I realize now that she was very ill and facing her illness with the kind of faith and courage that I haven't encountered since her death. I haven't seen my grandmother for eighteen years, but time has done nothing to change my firm belief that she loved me, and that if she was still alive, she would love me even more. I also have no doubt that she would be proud of me and what I've accomplished.

In a perfect world, she would still be here to tell me all these things and to help me through the tough times that come with just being alive. I may long for her presence, but I can't help but be grateful for those three years and the wonderful memories that came out of them. I feel eternally blessed to have known her at all.

Gabriel Ricard

She openeth her mouth with wisdom; and in her tongue is the law of kindness.

—Proverbs 31:26

Chapter Five

An Orange Blossom for Wisdom

Most of us have peeled an aromatic orange and enjoyed the sweet and delicious fruit inside, but few of us associate this luscious treat with the millions of tiny white flowers that perfume the orange groves every spring.

We've included the orange blossom in our bouquet to represent wisdom, one of the many qualities our grandmothers possess in great abundance. Like the love she bears forw her grandchildren, she shares ample offerings of her experience and insight without condition or price. And just as the heady fragrance of the orange blossom persists in our memory, our grandmother's precious gift remains to guide us in our journey through life.

Grandmothers possess a quality and quantity of wisdom often associated with people who have devoted a lifetime to learning—the professor with a wall full of diplomas or a Nobel-prize-winning scientist. Even though many grandmothers have attended college, and some may hold an honored position at a college or other facility where knowledge is held in high esteem, their greatest wisdom comes from quite a different source.

It comes from their unshakeable faith and from following their dreams and carrying on even when those dreams weren't fulfilled. It comes from facing each day as it came and learning from their mistakes. And, most significantly, it comes from recognizing the important things in life and living their life by them.

Scenes from an Amazing Life

While I was growing up, my father told me a few things about his mother, but my acquaintance with Maidie Armstrong really began during long conversations with my Aunt Helen, Maidie's only daughter. The things I discovered about my grandmother put me in awe of this remarkable woman, but it also left me with a profound sense of regret for not taking the time to ask my questions while she was still alive, and hear her extraordinary story in her own words.

I consoled myself with the thought that she may not have been comfortable talking about herself. Despite a loving, generous nature, I came to know her as a woman who preferred to keep her strongest emotions inside. She would have been more than happy to relate the events of her life, but the feelings involved in those events? Those may have been too difficult for her to share.

Wisdom has been defined as something that can't be taught, but acquired only through experience. If this is true, then my grandmother was one of the wisest people I have ever known.

After talking with my father and, later, with my Aunt Helen, I came to the conclusion that my grandmother never tried to avoid or run from the obstacles that she met on her journey through life. Instead, she viewed them as opportunities to learn something new.

When my grandfather was forced to retire from his work as a teamster because of a heart condition, my grandmother took on various jobs to keep the family fed and housed. During World War II, she became a foster mother. Newborn babies were brought to her home, where she cared for them until they were adopted.

My grandfather set up a room at the back of the house where up to twelve babies slept in two rows of cribs. My Aunt Helen, expecting her first child, came to live with my grandparents during this time, while her husband fought overseas with the Canadian Armed Forces.

When Aunt Helen first told me about the babies, I was amazed. "How did she look after them all?" I asked, remembering my own feelings of exhaustion caring for just one baby.

"Oh, she didn't just look after them," Aunt Helen replied. "She cared for those babies as if they were her own. Every day, depending on the weather, she bathed and dressed them all and took them outside. She played with them, talked to them, and she was always singing to them. Your grandfather and I helped out as much as we could—he diapered the babies and washed their bottles—but she did most of it on her own."

I tried to imagine sinks full of bottles, mountains of cloth diapers, and night after night of little or no sleep, and I couldn't. But I had no trouble picturing my grandmother holding those babies, smoothing their silky fine hair, and examining their tiny hands. I couldn't help but wonder about the babies and how their lives turned out. I do know that their journey began in a wonderful home blessed by the touch of my grandmother's loving arms.

Besides providing foster care for babies, my grandmother also found employment as a personal shopper. People would phone her with a specific list of things they wanted to buy, and she would go to the store, purchase the items, and deliver them. My talks with Aunt Helen introduced me to a woman who met life's difficulties head on. There wasn't time for self-pity or longing for a different set of circumstances. Like most of us, I'm sure there were moments when she felt discouraged or overwhelmed by her many responsibilities. I'm sure she missed the days when my grandfather had a job, not because it made her life easier in any way, but because it meant he was well enough to work.

After my grandfather died, Maidie went to work at a veterans' hospital. There she met her second husband, Jack. They married after Jack's recovery and, faced with finding a way to earn a living, they bought a neglected motel and orchard in the Okanagan area of British Columbia, Canada, a place known around the world for its beaches and abundant crops of fruit. Both in their sixties, they went to work fixing up their new investment. When Aunt Helen described how my grandmother mastered the use a cement mixer to build a wall around the property, I found myself, once again, deeply impressed by a woman who didn't let anything stop her from achieving her goals.

After many weeks, they were the proud owners of a modest, yet attractive, motel, complete with gas station and diner, and acres of fruit trees, nurtured and coaxed back to their former productivity. Word quickly spread that their motel was an economical, clean, and friendly place to stay and the "No Vacancy" sign became a familiar sight. The parking lot was usually filled with truck drivers who had made a special stop to enjoy my grandmother's goodies, including cakes, pies, cinnamon buns, and homemade soups.

This is the period of my grandmother's life that I recall most clearly. Every summer, my family would travel to Summerland, British Columbia, for a two-week holiday. I would tell my friends that I was going to visit my "Grandma in the Mountains." The area surrounding my grandparents' motel was not, by any stretch of the imagination, mountainous, but the rolling hills were very different from the flat prairie that I was used to.

My grandmother treated us like honored guests. We went to the beach every day, and I recall asking my father to carry me across the hot sand to the water's edge. I also remember my brother telling me that the Okanagan lake was full of fish with sharp teeth that would bite my toes if I let them hang over the edge of the air mattress. My grandmother usually packed a lunch for us to take, and she always had a delicious dinner waiting for us when we returned. I wish she could have joined us during our day trips to the beach or other places of amusement, but she had her hands full with caring for her guests and running the diner.

During our stay, we slept in the cool basement. Okanagan summers were hot, and there was no air conditioning. Quite often I would wake early and catch a glimpse of my grandmother tiptoeing to the freezer to retrieve meat or desserts to thaw for one of our meals during the day. Later I would watch as she drove an elderly Volkswagen piled high with clean linens, stopping at each motel unit to prepare it for the next guest. She appeared to possess an inexhaustible energy, and the only time I saw her sit down was after the evening meal. Even then, her hands kept busy with needlework or mending.

It was when we left for home that I saw a glimmer of the feelings she kept bottled up inside. As we packed up the car and said our good-byes, she would stand with her arms folded by the door. She said little, but her eyes would fill with tears. I may have been a young child, but her obvious emotion moved me deeply. I wanted to hug her and tell her we would be back, but her silence and body language prevented me from doing so.

My last clear remembrance of my grandmother was when my first child, Gabriel, was only six weeks old. I had traveled to see my parents and, since my grandparents lived only a few blocks away, I took the baby for a visit. In the photo I took of my grandmother holding Gabriel, her hand is resting tenderly on his head and her eyes, full of wonder and love, are fixed on his tiny face. You wouldn't know, to look at the picture, that Gabriel was only one of a multitude of babies she had held over the years. For that moment, as she cradled him in her arms, he was the most important person in the world.

I doubt that my grandmother ever knew how much wisdom she passed on to me—wisdom that I will, in turn, pass on to my children. But I have no doubt whatsoever that I am a better person for having known her.

If God had intended us to follow recipes,
he wouldn't have given us grandmothers.

—Linda Henley

My Grandmother—My Teacher

Throughout school and college, I was blessed with many wonderful teachers. I gained knowledge and skills from friends and coworkers, but the greatest lessons I ever learned came from a woman who never finished high school and never saw the inside of a college.

Like so many others struggling through the Great Depression, my grandmother, Virginia Sharp, had to quit school in the eighth grade to help bring money into the household. Sometimes she'd laugh and say, "You know, the 'good old days' weren't so good for a lot of people." But she never complained. She grew up surrounded by people with few possessions, no money, and little food, but those terrible times taught her something about life—something that made her a teacher with valuable lessons to share.

She never lectured or preached. Her lessons came from the way she lived. If a clerk at the store gave her too much change, she gave it back, even when there was barely enough money to pay for the groceries. "I can't keep what ain't mine," she would say, as we left the store. On the rare occasions that she received a bonus at work or came into an unexpected windfall, she insisted on sharing it with the family and kept little, if any, for herself. "There ain't nothing I want or nothing I need," she would tell us. "Go get yourselves something with it."

While the lessons about integrity, honesty, and generosity were important, there was one quality about my grandmother that stood out above all others. She was always there for her family and friends, and she loved them unconditionally. When I tried to tell her how much she meant to me, true to her nature, she shrugged it off. "Aw, son, I ain't done nothing," she said. "I'm just proud of how you turned out."

My grandmother may think that she hasn't done anything special, but I know differently. She's been an influence on my life—and me—as great as any other. I'm proud of you too, Granny—more than you'll ever know.

Steven Sharp

And so our mothers and grandmothers
have, more often than not anonymously,
handed on the creative spark, the seed
of the flower they themselves never hoped
to see—or like a sealed letter they could
not plainly read.

—Alice Walker

A Vacation to Remember

When I was sixteen, I knew my grandmother had a wealth of experience—an abundance that she would have eagerly shared—but I never took enough time to fully discover the riches she had to offer. Perhaps I thought, as young people often do, that there would always be time. Or maybe, suffering from teenage ignorance and arrogance, I didn't think I needed to be taught anything. In later years, I realized how wrong I had been, but it was too late. My best friend, Debbie, was much luckier than I was, although she certainly didn't think so at first.

All Debbie and I wanted to do was ride our horses, go to the beach, and spend time with our other friends. As summer vacation neared, we were full of plans. And then Debbie's parents told her she would be spending the first two weeks of August with them visiting her grandmother. Like a prisoner facing a life sentence, Debbie was horrified by the prospect of spending two long weeks at her grandmother's. Without her horse, her boyfriend, or me, she knew it would be little more than fourteen days of endless boredom.

Debbie did her best to change her parents' minds but nothing worked, and at the beginning of August we said our farewells as though two weeks had suddenly become two years. The only bright spot on a very dark horizon was the fact that her parents had told her that she could phone me when she got lonely.

She phoned me the day they got there and the next day, too. She told me that things were just as dull as she knew they would be. There was nothing to do and nowhere to go, and her grandmother didn't even have cable television. "I've already finished one of the books I brought, I've looked through every magazine in the house, and I've run out of things to tell my grandmother about my life," she said. "I'm not going to make it twelve more days."

I didn't hear from her the next day, or the day after that, and when she finally called, I expected her to be desperate. Instead, she told me she had been busy. "Doing what?" I asked in a bewildered voice.

"Oh, just stuff. With my grandmother."

When I pressed her for details, she said that it was kind of hard to explain. "My grandmother is pretty interesting," she said, "and she's even found me a place where I can ride." She promised to tell me about it when she got home. She called me a few more times, but our conversations were brief and, more puzzling yet, she sounded downright cheerful.

The rest of the time passed slowly for me, but Debbie finally came home and, as promised, told me all about her trip. On the afternoon of the third day, her parents went out to visit one of her mother's friends from school. Debbie didn't want to go because it sounded even less entertaining than staying behind. She was sitting in the living room watching one of the two television channels when her grandmother asked her if she'd like to help bake some cookies.

Feeling confused, I interrupted. "You baked cookies?" I asked. "And that was exciting?"

"It wasn't the cookies," Debbie replied, "although I did kind of want to know how my grandmother made her famous peanut butter chocolate chip cookies, and I was definitely ready for some junk food." She shook her head. "I told you it was hard to explain. We had a lot of fun making those cookies. We laughed and goofed around and ate a bunch of cookie dough. Just like that time you and I made those cookies that turned out so awful."

While the cookies were baking, her grandmother went up to the attic and brought down a bunch of old photo albums and a box full of other stuff. She and Debbie spent the rest of the afternoon going through the pictures. "My grandmother looked a lot like me when she was sixteen," Debbie told me. "Except she was prettier. And she showed me pictures of her horse and the ribbons she won in shows. My parents told me she had a horse when she was younger, but I never really paid attention."

"Wow," I said. I began to understand why Debbie's holiday had turned out better than we had both imagined.

"And the next day," Debbie continued, "she took me to see a friend who lived on a farm. He had two horses and told me I could ride whenever I wanted. And guess what?"

"What?"

"My grandmother actually went riding with me, and she's still pretty good. We had a great time."

I recall sitting there with Debbie that day long ago, sharing her feelings of amazement. Life—and grandmothers—certainly had a funny way of working out. It wasn't until years later, when we were both women with families of our own, that we revisited that summer, and Debbie tried, once more, to explain what had made that vacation so remarkable.

"It may sound weird," she said, "but it was making the cookies that helped me understand that my grandmother was a real person and not just my father's mother. I found out that I enjoyed her company and wanted to hear what she had to say. It was the photos, though, that proved to me how truly incredible she was. There was a lifetime of stories in those photo albums," she continued, "and all of the stories were fascinating. I felt overwhelmed by everything my grandmother had done and everything she knew."

"Remember how we thought those two weeks would never end?" I asked.

Debbie smiled. "You know, I've taken trips to all sorts of terrific places and don't remember much of anything, but I can recall that time with my grandmother as if it happened yesterday. I think it may have been the best vacation I ever had."

His lord said unto him, Well done, thou good and faithful servant: thou hast been faithful over a few things, I will make thee ruler over many things: enter thou into the joy of thy lord.

—Matthew 25:21

Chapter Six

A Scarlet Zinnia for Faithfulness

With over a hundred varieties in a diversity of colors and sizes, the zinnia has long been a favorite among gardeners. Enthusiasts can choose from an artist's palette of colors that includes white, cream, green, yellow, apricot, orange, red, bronze, crimson, purple, and lilac. The blooms can be striped, speckled, or bi-colored, and there are zinnias with double, semi-double, and dahlia-like "pompon" blooms. From dwarf plants that don't exceed six inches in height to beauties that can reach three feet, there is a size to suit every landscaping need.

We've selected the scarlet zinnia to represent faithfulness. In this uncertain world where temporary, superficial relationships are too often the norm, a grandmother remains a constant. We seek refuge in her unwavering loyalty, secure in the knowledge that she will love us even when we feel as though no one else does. Even when we don't love ourselves.

Faithfulness

For many of us, our grandmothers have been a constant on our roller-coaster ride through life. The black-and-white photo of a beaming woman holding a newborn baby survives as proof that she was right there from the beginning. Our grandmothers are intrinsically connected to our earliest memories. We may not recall the faces too clearly in those memories, but we will never forget the soothing words and loving arms. And, as we grew up and struggled through a multitude of changes, we came to count on our grandmothers' steady and stable presence.

Our grandmothers' faithfulness had its start long before we were born. The moment these women became mothers—like anyone committed to a life's work—they signed up for the duration. There would be no resignation and no retirement, and that's exactly the way they wanted it. They knew we would need a shelter from the storms that came our way, and they were always there, ready and willing, to provide it.

Once a Mother, Always a Mother

I was almost forty years old when I gave birth to my fourth child, Connor. During my brief stay in the hospital, I shared a room with three other women. Privacy was at a premium, and I couldn't help but notice that my roommates' mothers were women close to my own age. There I was, cradling my son at the beginning of a long journey that would take him to adulthood, while the new grandmothers around me stood on the brink of quite a different adventure. Part of me envied them.

I was right in the middle of raising Connor's three siblings, and it was the most difficult job I had ever undertaken. My children were, without a doubt, the best things that had ever happened to me, but I wondered what it would be like to be a grandmother. I saw grandmothers as having things on their own terms. They had the party without having to prepare for it or clean up after it was over. Although this may have been true for some women, I soon found out that, for other grandmothers, it was a completely different story.

It wasn't until I moved to Virginia and started attending church that I discovered a very special type of grandmother. One of the things that appealed to me about the church was the size of the congregation. Only about forty people attended regularly, and they seemed more like a large extended family than a congregation.

I spent my first weeks at church feeling shy and hesitant, but I longed to share in the caring and closeness I witnessed every Sunday. I had never been much of a joiner, but these people had something I wanted. It took a while to get the names straight and remember which children belonged to which parents, but thanks to the warm and welcoming attitude surrounding me, my comfort level quickly increased.

There were two women who attended church every Sunday with their grandchildren. Hazel was always accompanied by her two granddaughters, Mia and Chloe, and Doris brought her grandson, Ryan. At first, I assumed the children lived with their parents and came to church with their grandmothers as part of a weekend visit. It wasn't long, however, before I discovered that Mia, Chloe, and Ryan were not visitors in their grandmothers' homes, but permanent residents. Both Hazel and Doris had undertaken the responsibility of raising their grandchildren.

This somewhat unconventional situation reminded me of a conversation I once had with my mother. She and a friend had been talking about their children, and my mother's friend made it perfectly clear that once her children left home, they no longer had the option of returning for anything more than a visit. My mother strongly disagreed with her friend's attitude. "Once a mother, always a mother," she told me. "Even when your children are grown, they are still your children." Like my mother, Doris and Hazel believed that the responsibility of parenthood didn't end when their children walked out the door to start their own lives.

Although we never discussed it, I knew both women had made their choices without debate or deliberation. When their grandchildren needed a home, they stepped forward without hesitation to provide that home. At a time when most women had said farewell to monsters in the closet, toys scattered throughout the house, and soccer games in the rain, Hazel and Doris had agreed to a repeat performance. And after several years of watching them with their grandchildren, it's abundantly clear that neither one of them has ever regretted her decision.

It was women like Doris and Hazel who changed my stereotypical view of grandmothers. They helped me realize that grandmothers aren't simply women whose children have started their own family. Some grandmothers are women who prove their lifelong commitment to motherhood by doing whatever they can to help their children, even if it means becoming a mother all over again. Women like Hazel and Doris deserve a standing ovation. They've earned it.

A child needs a grandparent, anybody's grandparent, to grow a little more securely into an unfamiliar world.

—Charles and Ann Morse

Learning to Say Goodbye

When I was a little girl, my family lived just across a field from my grandparents' house. I was only two when my Papa Moses died and, even though I was very young, I knew Granny was having a hard time. So, when I was about three, I told my mom I was going to live with Granny so she wouldn't have to be alone. Granny loved the idea and, since my mom knew she would see me all the time, she said I could go. My family had supper at Granny's almost every night. My granny loved to cook, and she loved to dance.

Then, Granny met Leroy. They dated for a while and became engaged. We were all so happy for them, but before they could get married, Leroy died, and Granny was alone again. This time, my sister and I often stayed with her so she wouldn't be lonely. Granny was strong and, just as she learned to live again after my grandfather's death, eventually she began to feel better after Leroy died.

The time went by, and Granny kept busy. She started going to dances, and that's where she met Tom. They began to see each other often and decided to get married. Granny decided to move to the town where Tom lived and, just like that, she wasn't across the field anymore. I went from seeing her every day to visiting her once a month, or even once every two months. I missed her so much. When Tom and Granny started to come to our church every Sunday, it made me very happy.

When Granny found out she had cancer, she went through surgery, chemotherapy, and radiation. Right before Christmas, the doctors told her the cancer was gone. To celebrate, we took her to South Carolina to visit her ten brothers and sisters, and they all had a wonderful time. We had no way of knowing that it would be her last trip.

In the middle of January, the doctors told her that the cancer had returned. So she endured more radiation. It wasn't long before she had to be admitted to the hospital for pain management. The doctors told my mother that Granny had only six weeks to live. My mother never told me, but, somehow, I knew. My granny went through so much before she died, but she never complained. She was too busy worrying about everyone else. In the days just before she died, she wasn't in much pain, but she knew where she was, and she knew where she was going. She believed that she was on her way to see Papa Moses, Leroy, and her parents.

When I think back to when she first moved away, I remember how horrible I felt, but now I realize that God knew exactly what He was doing. He was slowly taking her out of my life, so I would be more prepared for the day when she wouldn't be here. I can't imagine how I would have felt if she had died during the time we lived so close together.

It's taken me a long time, but I know she's in a better place. I also know that I'll see her someday because her spirit will live on for eternity.

Brandy Blythe

Grandma always made you feel she had been waiting to see just you all day and now the day was complete.

—Marcy DeMaree

In My Nana's World

In the dreamy, private domain that I inhabited as a child, I used books to help me make sense of the world around me, and I loved knowing my nana was one of the good grandmothers that I read about. There were a great many of us grandchildren, but I felt no longing to be her favorite. I received all the comfort I needed from imagining that my nana was just like the women in my beloved stories.

Like those characters, she had fluffy white hair, permed and curled regularly, and always wore a flowered housedress and fresh apron. She spent her days involved in a myriad of household tasks, a blur of busyness that ended only when her health deteriorated. I don't remember being cuddled or having long chats with her. Her reassuring presence and familiar physical appearance provided all the security I needed.

My family lived just two doors away, and we spent much of our time at Nana's. Her home was an odd combination of the comforting and the mysterious. The front was "out of bounds," used by family who came to stay, and I don't remember ever going up the hallway and into those front bedrooms. It never bothered me, though, because the heart of Nana's home was the kitchen with the old wood stove and the big wooden table with the bowl of freshly baked scones sitting in the middle of it.

I can still see her out in her vegetable garden, surrounded by plum, pear, and apple trees. In spring, I had to walk under the snowball tree—my "pom-pom" tree—in order to reach the toilet and, as if in a sudden snow flurry, I often found myself dusted with the blossoms that invariably fell. The trellis between the kitchen door and laundry door was covered with vines, and every night brought a visit from Nana's possum, his two eyes providing an eerie glow in the black night.

I wanted to do something special for Nana, so one day I decided to cover all her books in brown paper and plastic. I labeled them and returned them, neatly arranged, to the shelves. Libraries kept their books covered in plastic that kept them from being damaged, so by covering Nana's books, I saved them from further deterioration.

I loved her books, as I loved all books, and by taking care of her books, I wanted to show Nana that I loved her, too. When she bought all that brown paper and plastic for me, she gave my ideas and efforts value. And when she shared in my satisfaction and pride, she showed me how much she loved me.

Like much of my past, my memories of Nana have been blurred by the passage of many years. What remains crystal clear, however, is my realization that she was far more than a character out of my wonderful stories. She nurtured and valued the fantasies of my youth, and that left me with a sense of importance for which I will always be grateful.

Rosalie Franklin

Chapter Seven

A Gladiolus for Love at First Sight

You only have to see a bouquet of spectacular and stately gladioli to understand why this is one of the most popular garden flowers. It's also easy to see why, with its unique spike of blossoms, the gladiolus was once known as the sword lily. Gladioli are easy to plant and require a minimum of care, making them an ideal choice for the amateur gardener. Plant the corms at two-week intervals and you can enjoy their splendid blooms all summer long.

The gladiolus in our bouquet represents "love at first sight," and our grandmothers are living proof that this romantic phenomenon exists. Ask the woman who has just seen her newborn grandson for the first time to describe the baby, and she will answer without hesitation. "He is the most beautiful baby in the world."

Love at First Sight Introduction

Love at first sight is one of those topics that provoke a variety of opinions. Some insist it's merely a romantic notion or physical reaction. There are scientists who measure brain activity and claim it's possible, but only if certain psychological and circumstantial criteria are met.

However, ask a grandmother who has just seen her grandchild for the first time if love at first sight exists, and you will most likely hear a resounding yes. Given the opportunity, these women will explain that they are well acquainted with the phenomenon. The birth of their own child, years before, made them firm believers, and the arrival of their grandchild only serves as a reminder that love at first sight, like miracles, happens every day.

Waiting for Emily

When my first child, Gabriel, was about eighteen months old, my husband found work in one of the logging communities on Vancouver Island. We had been living in Alberta, Canada, about 600 miles from my parents. The separation had been hard on everyone, but more than anything, I had missed sharing the first exciting months of my son's life with his grandparents. When I discovered we would be living about half an hour's drive from their home, I was ecstatic.

My parents had seen Gabriel only twice. My mother had been ill most of my life with chronic asthma, and her health problems had prevented her and my father from being with me when the baby was born. However, when Gabriel was only six weeks old, he and I took a plane trip to meet his grandparents. Then, remarkably, as we began to plan for Gabriel's first birthday, my mother's health improved to the point where she and my father were able to join the celebration.

My mother and father had started their journey as grandparents with some ambivalence, but they had grown to love Gabriel as only grandparents can, and they were as excited about our move as we were. They would finally have the opportunity to be more than just visitors, and Gabriel would reap the blessings of having loving family close by. I realized that my mother's physical participation in Gabriel's life would be limited by her asthma, but I also knew, without a doubt, that her emotional contribution would be endless.

Gabriel loved spending time with his grandparents. He soon learned that Grandpa was always available to answer his questions and would never turn down the invitation to "Read me a story, Grandpa." Grammy, as my mother decided she would like to be called, loved to read, too, but her real area of expertise was cuddling. And when the inevitable bumps, scrapes, and other mishaps occurred, Grammy had the magic to make it all better.

I remember Gabriel on his grandmother's lap one evening long ago, her head inclined slightly to hear his whispered secrets, her arms wrapped around his tiny body. Abruptly, he fell silent, his head nestled against her chest, and within seconds, he was asleep. Lulled by the hush of the now-quiet room, and by the gentle rhythm of Gabriel's breathing, my mother soon closed her eyes and fell asleep, too. I watched them sleep for a long time, and I recall thinking that I was the luckiest person in the world.

Just when I thought my happiness was complete, I discovered that I was going to have another baby. There was none of the anxiety and uncertainty with which I faced the news of my first pregnancy. This time, I felt only joy and excited anticipation, feelings that were shared by my husband and my parents, especially my mother. Almost immediately, she determined that my baby would be a girl, and because my husband was French-Canadian, she also decided that her new granddaughter should have a French name. She called me almost every morning and often, even before she said hello, she would tender her latest name suggestion. "What about Monique?" she might say, or, "How about Mariel?"

My pregnancy was a blessing for so many reasons, one of which was somewhat bittersweet. My mother's asthma had continued to worsen, and the side effects of the medicine she took to control it were causing serious problems. The prospect of a new grandchild, however, filled her with renewed strength to fight her illness and gave her something wonderful and miraculous to look forward to.

Once again, I was lucky enough to escape the misery of morning sickness and some of the other symptoms that plague so many mothers-to-be. However, I had gained over fifty pounds during my pregnancy with Gabriel and, although I lost it in the months following his birth, I dreaded the thought of piling on the pounds once more. What if I didn't lose the weight this time? What if the "beached whale" syndrome was permanent? When I confided my worries to my mother, she slipped into one of the many roles she would play in my life—that of my friend—and she took me to the mall to buy some new maternity clothes and get my hair done. I still couldn't resist checking out my rear "view" in the mirror on occasion, but, thanks to my mother, I faced the remainder of my pregnancy focused on having a healthy baby, and not my rapidly expanding waistline.

With my due date about two months away, another fear surfaced. My first labor had been long and difficult and left me trying to remember what misguided person told me that I would forget the pain of childbirth as soon as I saw my new baby. I hadn't forgotten a single contraction, and when I was about seven months pregnant, it all came back to haunt me with every detail intact. And then one day, during one of our countless cups of tea together, my mother demonstrated her skill as a mind reader.

For reasons I still can't fathom, she began to talk about her labor, first with my brother, and then with me. She explained that my brother had been born during a time when ultrasounds were nonexistent, and cesarean births were rare, and the fact that he was in a breech position wasn't discovered until she was well into hard labor. "I had a terrible time," she said, "and then four years later, when I found out I was going to have another baby, I was so scared."

"I'm scared, too," I whispered and then paused, startled that I had actually spoken the words out loud. "Sometimes, for a second or so, I even wish I could change my mind." My mother smiled in a way that told me she knew exactly how I felt. "How did you stop being afraid?" I asked finally.

"Oh, that was easy," she said. "Every time I felt a little anxious or worried, I would watch your brother sleep. It always made me feel as though I could accomplish anything." She shook her head. "I would never forget your brother's birth, but whenever I looked at him, I knew without a doubt it had all been worth it. Besides," she added, "I wanted another baby more than anything in the whole world."

I knew I had to ask. "And your labor with me?"

My mother snapped her fingers. "Like that," she said. "Afterwards, all I could talk about was getting something to eat. I was starved!"

The baby was due on New Year's Eve, but the doctor told me that I might be spending Christmas in the maternity ward. My mother had warned me that she had better be the first to know, so when my water broke at one o'clock in the morning on December 22, I phoned her. She and my father were going to meet us at the hospital and pick up Gabriel, now three years old.

While Gabriel vibrated with the excitement of having his first sleepover at Grammy and Grandpa's house, I began to experience stronger and more regular contractions. I also hoped my parents would arrive soon. Not only was I eager to relinquish my responsibility for a rambunctious three-year-old, I was looking forward to seeing my mother. The disappointment of her missing Gabriel's birth had vanished long ago, replaced by the joy of knowing that she was on her way to be with me. Although she wouldn't be attending the actual birth, she would be there to see and hold her new grandchild shortly after the baby was born.

At last they appeared, my mother radiant with excitement and my father, bleary-eyed and muttering good-naturedly about being woken up in the middle of the night. Of course, my mother wanted to stay and wait for her granddaughter's—she still insisted the baby was a girl—debut, but my father argued that they should go home. "Gabriel needs to get some sleep," he said. He put his arm around my mother. "And your back is really bothering you. Come to think of it, all three of us should go home and get some sleep."

I looked at my mother. She was still beaming, but then I saw the lines of fatigue and pain I hadn't noticed when she first arrived. I persuaded her to leave and promised to call as soon as I could.

Three hours after they left, Emily Charlotte Monique was born. With my new daughter in my arms, I made my way to the pay phone down the hall. My mother answered on the first ring. "I have someone here waiting to meet her grandparents," I said.

"Her?" my mother replied. "I knew it!"

And then suddenly, she and my father were there at the door to my room. "I'm a big brother," Gabriel announced in a voice loud enough for the entire floor to hear, and we all laughed. My mother hurried to my bedside, and I gently transferred the baby to her eager arms. "Oh," she said quietly, and her eyes filled with tears. "She's so tiny." Then I watched as my mother lowered her head and whispered in the baby's ear. "I'm your Grammy," she said, "and I love you."

A mother becomes a true grandmother the day she stops noticing the terrible things her children do because she is so enchanted with the wonderful things her grandchildren do.

—Lois Wyse

Remembering Granny

My granny was a very influential part of my life. Our family has been through many trials and tribulations, but I will always remember Granny because she was so strong. She loved everyone—her daughters, her grandchildren, her first husband, whom we called Papa Moses, her second husband, whose name is Thomas, her four sisters, and her five brothers. That's just her family. She loved practically everyone else, too.

I remember spending the night with Granny. I used to tell my momma that I wanted to sleep over at Granny's, so she would phone and Granny always told me to hurry over. When we got to Granny's, she would have dinner ready for everyone. When it was time for bed, she always told me a story, and I went right to sleep.

I think my granny made the people around her stronger, too. When she was suffering from a terminal illness, I gave my Aunt Anne—Granny's sister—a nickname. I called her Nanny Annie because she took care of my granny, my sister and me, and my cousins. And then, when we were at Granny's funeral, I started crying, and my Uncle Donald—Granny's brother—hugged me and told me Granny was with God. I didn't want to let Granny go, but I didn't want her to suffer anymore. I miss her every single day. She made me so happy—Rest in peace, Granny!

Jennifer Blythe

A grandmother pretends she doesn't know who you are on Halloween.

—Erma Bombeck

But the fruit of the Spirit is love, joy, peace, longsuffering, gentleness, goodness, faith, meekness, [and] temperance. . . .

—Galatians 5:22–23

Chapter Eight

A Forget-Me-Not for Enduring Memories

The dainty forget-me-not is an excellent choice for the gardener desiring a ground cover of lovely flowers that spread naturally. And because it represents enduring memories, this charming bloom is also perfect for our grandmother's bouquet.

We are often too preoccupied to remember much of anything. Always busy and sometimes stressed, we may even have trouble recalling what we ate for breakfast, but at the mention of our grandmothers, we will smile and launch into a litany of memories. Events from long ago remain untarnished by time and are so easily recalled, perhaps because they are such an integral part of who we've become.

Every time we hum her favorite song, or bake the cookies she always had waiting for us when we came to visit, we pay homage to Grandmother and the precious memories she created.

Enduring Memories

We might not be able to remember what we had for lunch, but regularly, and often without warning, memories make their presence known. Perhaps it's a song on the radio, or a handwritten recipe stuck between the pages of a cookbook. It might be a photograph discovered at the bottom of a drawer, or simply a date on the calendar. Whatever the cue may be, vivid and perfectly preserved memories freeze the moment and take us on a trip back in time.

These memories come equipped with all five senses. We can hear the sound of our father's voice the night we missed our curfew and smell the fresh bread our grandmother baked every day. We can see our baby's first smile, taste the liver our mother insisted that we try just once, and feel the smoothness of our baby's cheek.

Memories may bring heartache but, more often than not, they make it possible for us to remember the people who blessed our lives and to revisit the moments we wouldn't have missed for anything.

Mustard Pickles

My father is truly his mother's son. He is a quiet, reserved man with a delightful sense of humor, but he rarely displays deep emotion. My grandmother was much the same way—the only time I saw her cry was when we said good-bye after spending our holidays with her and my grandfather. Even then, she didn't really cry, but her eyes would fill with tears. I suspect if I had hugged her and told her not to cry, she would have gently released herself from my arms and insisted that it was only a speck of dust causing her tears.

I saw my father cry only once and, again, it involved saying good-bye. I was teaching school about 300 miles from my hometown, and my parents had come to visit me. When the time came for them to leave, my father took me in his arms and much to my shock and dismay, I felt his shoulders shaking with sobs.

I take after my mother. I cry frequently and effortlessly and get angry just as easily, although, like a match, my tears and fury sputter and die quickly. I now realize that both my father and grandmother had their share of frustration and sadness but, unlike me, they kept it all locked inside. When my grandmother died, I expected my father to cry. After all, she was his mother, and I never doubted his deep affection for her. I loved watching them together. He obviously adored her, and sometimes his marvelous, dry sense of humor made her laugh out loud. I will always remember the sound of that laughter, and the self-conscious silence that followed. She simply wasn't comfortable expressing herself emotionally, but I didn't care. I knew the feelings were there, and I knew they came from her heart.

I didn't see my father cry when she died. Nothing he did or said indicated that he had undergone a life-changing experience. Perhaps he did his grieving in private, I thought. It wasn't as though I wanted to see him cry, but I had hoped that the tears might trigger a desire for him to talk. I had little interest in the places, names, and dates that I already knew, but I wanted to hear about his childhood—to know my father as the boy he once was. Just as he was part of me genetically, in some strange way I saw those recollections as being part of me, too.

Time passed, however, and her name was rarely mentioned. I missed her terribly, and I was certain my father missed her, too, but he didn't say a word. The death of his mother meant that he was now the older generation, and I wondered if he might be coming to terms with his own mortality. I certainly didn't expect him to suddenly burst forth with a lengthy discourse on the loss of his mother, but I longed to share my grief and perhaps lessen the pain by doing so.

A few months later we all gathered for a family dinner. My brother and his family came from Vancouver, and my mother prepared a wonderful meal. She loved to entertain, and it was a delight to sit in the dining room at a table covered with linen, eating and drinking from dishes reserved for special occasions. At some point during the meal, I noticed my father staring at the table. I wondered if I had forgotten something. "Can I get you anything, Dad?" I asked.

He shook his head, and then he looked up at me. He may have been smiling, but his eyes spoke of bittersweet memories. "I was just thinking how good your grandmother's mustard pickles would taste with this pot roast," he said. He was right. Without Grandma's mustard pickles, the meal wasn't complete.

No one said anything for a few minutes. Finally, my father spoke again. "I guess we won't be getting any more mustard pickles." It was a remark typical of his dry humor, and we all burst out laughing. I recalled the laughter at my grandmother's table, and when I looked over at my father, I saw the telltale glimmer of tears in his eyes. He caught my glance, and it was then I knew how much he missed her.

I realized that the mustard pickles represented the hundreds of moments and memories that had been laid to rest with his beloved mother. These recollections would be resurrected time and again to keep her alive in our hearts and minds, but they would carry the sting of reminding us that she was really gone. That night, long after the meal was finished and the plates cleared, we talked about Grandma Armstrong. Later I asked my mother to write out the recipe for mustard pickles. I vowed to make them someday, but, worried that they wouldn't be as good as my grandmother's, I never did. Maybe I should give it a try. I think my grandmother would be pleased.

The history of our grandparents is remembered not with rose petals but in the laughter and tears of their children and their children's children. It is into us that the lives of the grandparents have gone. It is in us that their history becomes a future.

—Charles and Ann Morse

Grandchildren Spark Memories of Summers Long Ago

Summer has come, and the grandchildren will soon be here. If you are a grandmother, you know that they bring the blessing of renewal. The world becomes fresh and exciting through their eyes, ears, and noses. They taste and touch with wonder. They restore our senses as well as our souls. Anticipating their arrival, I have found myself recalling the childhood summers I spent with my own grandparents.

In the days before air conditioning, city summers were punishing, so my parents took me to the Virginia countryside every summer. Fortunately for me, both sets of grandparents lived in Sussex County.

My earliest memory is being met at the Petersburg train station by my mother's father—the only grandparent who drove a car. Although he died when I was eight, I still can see his kind face light up as he collected us and piled our luggage into his ancient black Ford. I can smell the cigar smoke in the car (the only place he could smoke, since Gran did not allow cigars in the house). As the wind blew through an open window into my gritty face, I stared at the incredible greenery bathed in twilight. It was a welcome relief from the blocks of hot cement we had left behind in Philadelphia.

Since it was always dark by the time we arrived at the farm, I could only hear the enticing sounds of the country—the peepers at the branch, the katydids, the whippoorwills, and the tree frogs. I was impatient to kick off my shoes and run through the soft grass to visit the farm animals, so my usual bedtime prayer ended with a special request. "Please let me go to sleep fast so morning will come soon."

From those days long ago, before anyone worried about cholesterol, I can still taste the soft biscuits made with lard, running red with homemade plum jam, the fried apples and ham Gran served with them. She took me to pick wild blackberries and showed me how to track a guinea hen and find the small brown eggs. She taught me to look down and find the busy ant colonies and tiny toads. She taught me to look up and discover cloud formations with human and animal shapes. She instilled in a small child a deeper respect for all creation.

Just for me, Granddad always fixed a fresh sand pile, mounded around a tall oak in the back yard. Under that tree, I became an architect of castles and frog houses shaped around my small feet. Under another tree, a swing waited. Granddad had made it from an oak slab and hung it from stout ropes. I knew I could trust Granddad by the care he had taken in building my swing.

Visits to my other grandparents' farm held different pleasures. Mom, as everyone called my grandmother, would read to me—*The Secret Garden*, *Beautiful Joe*, *Black Beauty*, and the tales of Thornton Burgess—until she had, as she would say, "a frog in my throat." She guided me through her world of flowers, teaching me their names, diverse fragrances, colors, and shapes. She showed me how to find a drop of honey in the honeysuckle and allowed me to gently stroke the fuzzy caterpillar.

Grandpop would put me on Jill, the mule, and I would ride to the orchard, followed by watchful Jack, the old farm collie. All of Grandpop's animals would eat from his hand, and he had names for each of them. He would let me help him pull the buckets of cold water from the well to water them.

When our grandchildren come, we may rent Disney tapes, take them to Goochland Library for story time, or plan a trip to an amusement park. But we also will read to them, show them hummingbirds sipping from the bright, cuplike blooms in the kitchen garden, and take them to the secret place where the beavers dwell. We will watch the deer graze and treat the children to the spectacular light show the fireflies put on every night. We will try to give them memories of their own. I hope that they, too, will cherish those memories and revisit them with joy in the years to come.

Zella Spiers

Nobody can do for little children what grandparents do. Grandparents sort of sprinkle stardust over the lives of little children.

—Alex Haley

The Beginning of the Movie

A few nights ago, my husband, Tom, stayed up late to watch a movie. The next morning, I asked him if he had enjoyed the show, and a slightly embarrassed expression appeared on his face. "I fell asleep in the middle and woke up just in time to see the credits roll," he said and shook his head. "I've seen the beginning and ending of more movies than I can count."

I was reminded of our conversation this morning when I looked at my daughter, Emily. She will turn eighteen this December, and, like Tom with his movie, I remember the beginning so clearly. I recall holding her in my arms for the first time, those early weeks when she cried without stopping from five to seven every evening, and her penchant for shedding her clothes as soon as she stepped outside the back door. I can still feel her tiny body in my hands as I bathed her, I can still smell her hair, and I can still see her walking through the door of the kindergarten on her first day.

The little girl is gone, replaced by a young woman who will be on her own in a very short time. I struggle to remember her childhood but, as though someone pressed the fast-forward button on my life, much of it is a blur. And when I'm reminded that she will be an adult in a few months, I can't help but wish her grandmother had lived long enough to know the fine young lady that Emily has become. My mom died when Emily was only eight months old, but I have an abundance of sweet memories stored from that brief period—memories that I savor and cherish.

When I gave birth to a strong, healthy girl, three days before Christmas, everyone rejoiced. I marveled at Emily's head of silky black hair and her exquisite complexion, but within twenty-four hours, her skin had taken on a distinctly orange cast, and she looked more like a Halloween pumpkin than the porcelain doll we had welcomed the day before. Blood tests revealed that Emily and I had incompatible blood types, and plans were made to transport her to a larger hospital where a blood transfusion could be performed.

I panicked and phoned my mother. I didn't fully understand what was wrong, and I was scared to death. My mother kept the conversation brief. "Everything's going to be okay," she said. "I'll be waiting for you at the hospital." When the ambulance arrived, I was told I couldn't accompany the baby. Convinced I would never see my precious baby again, I sobbed as the nurse pried her out of my arms and handed her to the driver. As soon as the ambulance left, my husband and I were on our way, and when we got to the hospital, my mother was waiting, wearing a comforting smile. She held me for a few moments and repeated her mantra. "Everything's going to be okay," she said. "I just know it."

A short time later, we met with the pediatrician who carefully explained what the problem was and what he planned to do to correct it. He assured me that it was a very straightforward procedure, one that he had performed many times. He told us we would be able to see Emily in a few hours. "Why don't you go and have something to eat?" he said.

Was this man insane, I thought? How could I eat? "That's a wonderful idea," my mother said. "Let's go to the cafeteria." I looked at her as though she, too, had lost her mind, but I reluctantly accompanied her and my husband to the cafeteria. While the two of them enjoyed a full-course meal and talked nonstop, I silently nursed my coffee. Maybe my hormones decided to give me a break, because, as I sat there, it occurred to me that if my mother, my husband, and the doctor weren't overly concerned, perhaps I didn't need to be, either.

I looked across the table at my mother and she grinned. That smile banished any remnants of fear I might have been harboring, and I abruptly realized that I was hungry. "I'm going to get something to eat," I said.

"All right," my mother said, "but when you're done, let's go to the gift shop. I saw some cute little baby sweaters."

Five days later, on my parents' fortieth wedding anniversary, Emily came home from the hospital. We celebrated by having lunch at a favorite restaurant, and my mother introduced Emily, wearing her new sweater, to the entire staff and most of the other diners. I still have that tiny sweater, and I will never forget the smile that told me everything was going to be okay.

My One and Only Grandmother

My grandma was not my grandmother. She was my mother's aunt—my great-aunt—but in the absence of any living grandparents of our own, she served as a surrogate to my sister and me. She was the real grandmother to my two cousins who lived in New Jersey, about a half-hour's drive across the George Washington Bridge from our New York home.

Home to my grandma was a one-room garden apartment with a couch in the living room that converted into her bed, a small kitchen, and a large closet you passed through to get to the bathroom. Visits were always day trips. We'd park on the street and walk up the cement sidewalk to her front door, the farthest one from the road. After a short while, we'd all pile back in the car and drive over to the adjacent town where my cousins lived.

My cousins and I liked grandma's apartment, so different from our more traditional houses. We also liked that she was born in 1900, making it easy to calculate her age. Although she was just in her sixties, she was very gray, very wrinkled, and very dowdy in both dress and bodily shape. This is not just in memory. I have the pictures to prove it.

In the pictures, she looks like a traditional grandmother but, in real life, she didn't fit the mold. She couldn't cook. Once when I stayed overnight, we made beef stew, a meat and potato concoction boiled in water. Her baking wasn't any better. She served the same hard, tasteless dough balls she called sugar cookies whenever we saw her.

I saw her every month or two, and sometime during my teens became aware of our family lineage. She was the sister to my mother's father, the man whose wife was my true grandmother, a set of grandparents whose images were preserved in a few old sepia photographs. But my grandma was the only grandmother who'd ever instructed me in the kitchen, although she hated to cook, or attempted to teach me to crochet, a skill I couldn't master. Not being authentic did not make her any less real. She had no culinary abilities, but she fed me a lifetime of memories that would last.

The last picture I have of my grandma was taken in early 1981. She is sitting in my mother's living room chair cradling my newborn daughter in her arms. She looks frailer but otherwise as gray, wrinkled, and dowdy as I'll always remember her. She looks very grandmotherly.

Peggy Duffy

Our grandchildren accept us for ourselves, without rebuke or effort to change us, as no one in our entire lives has ever done, not our parents, siblings, spouses, friends – and hardly ever our own grown children.

—Ruth Goode

*Finally, brethren, whatsoever things
are true, whatsoever things are honest,
whatsoever things are just, whatsoever
things are pure, whatsoever things are
lovely, whatsoever things are of good
report; if there be any virtue, and if there
be any praise, think on these things.*

—Philippians 4:8

Epilogue

Closing Thoughts about Grandmothers

It has been almost twenty-two years since I became a mother and took the first hesitant steps of the most amazing journey of my life. I'd be a fool to dispute the passage of time, but part of me is astonished—and, I confess, a bit frightened—that so many years could slip by with so little effort. Like a tiny pebble tossed in the lake, the time has disappeared with barely a ripple.

While countless people have come and gone in my children's lives, my place in their hearts has remained secure. Someday soon, however, our dance together will end, and when the next song begins, they will be facing new partners—the ones they've chosen for the rest of their lives.

Like the other changes I've experienced as a mother, this one will have its bittersweet moments, but I'm confident that the smiles will far outnumber the tears. I welcome the opportunity to share my children's joy and their sorrow, if need be, as they start their own lives. I am delighted by the thought of our family growing to include their spouses. And I love the idea of becoming a grandmother. Grandchildren are like the paycheck you receive after working countless hours of overtime at the best job you've ever had.

Twenty-two years ago, I wondered if I would be a good mother, and because babies don't come with instructions, I suffered through many moments of anxiety and plain old panic. Those early months of my son's life were rife with crises, and I still have the stack of dog-eared books I consulted for every burp and every sniffle. It was my own mother, however, who gave me what I really needed.

Looking back, I realize it wasn't her words that made the difference. It was her silence. Her advice was readily available and eagerly shared—but only when I asked for it. By standing back and allowing me to find my own way, she gave me the chance to develop the self-confidence that would carry me through the challenges she knew were coming. She taught me to trust my instincts, and by raising me with unconditional love, she gave me the greatest gift of all. I'm not worried about whether or not I'll be a good grandmother. If I continue to rely on the legacy of life lessons my mother left behind, I have a feeling I'll do just fine.

Early last fall, I noticed that one of my young hens was sitting on her first clutch of eggs. I've always been impressed with the dedication of a hen determined to hatch out a brood of chicks, and this pullet was no exception. She rarely left her nest, and when she did, it was only to take in life-sustaining food and water.

One day, while I was feeding the chickens, I noticed her amongst the group scratching and eating at my feet. When I looked across the pen to her nest, I was surprised to see one of my older hens sitting on the eggs. Later, when I looked again, the pullet had resumed her position on the nest. The old hen remained close by, but it was obvious she had no intention of interfering with the younger bird. I was charmed by the thought that the older chicken was like a grandmother, standing by in case she was needed and stepping in when the pullet needed a break.

Grandmothers come in all shapes and sizes. Some have gray hair and wear pearls, while others have burgundy streaks and wear a nose ring. Some knit and others skydive. There are grandmothers who bake cookies and ones who burn toast. Despite these differences, they all have one thing in common—the opportunity to make a difference in their grandchildren's lives. I hope I make the most of that opportunity. I pray that I will have what it takes to stand back and let my children find their own way, to teach them to trust their instincts, and to leave a legacy of love that endures long after I'm gone.

About the Author

Susan B. Townsend, author of *A Bouquet for Mom,* is a writer and stay-at-home mother. She lives on a farm in southeastern Virginia with her husband, five children, and a menagerie of animals. Her work has appeared in *A Cup of Comfort® for Mothers and Daughters, A Cup of Comfort® for Teachers,* and *A Cup of Comfort® for Mothers to Be.* She is a contributing editor of *A Cup of Comfort® Book of Prayer* scheduled for release in Fall 2007. She can be reached at *monitor@visi.net.*

CPSIA information can be obtained
at www.ICGtesting.com
Printed in the USA
BVHW090826180121
598043BV00046B/2572